LEXINGTON PUBLIC LIBRARY

D1239089

All about POLICE OFFICERS

Mari Schuh

Lerner Publications ◆ Minneapolis

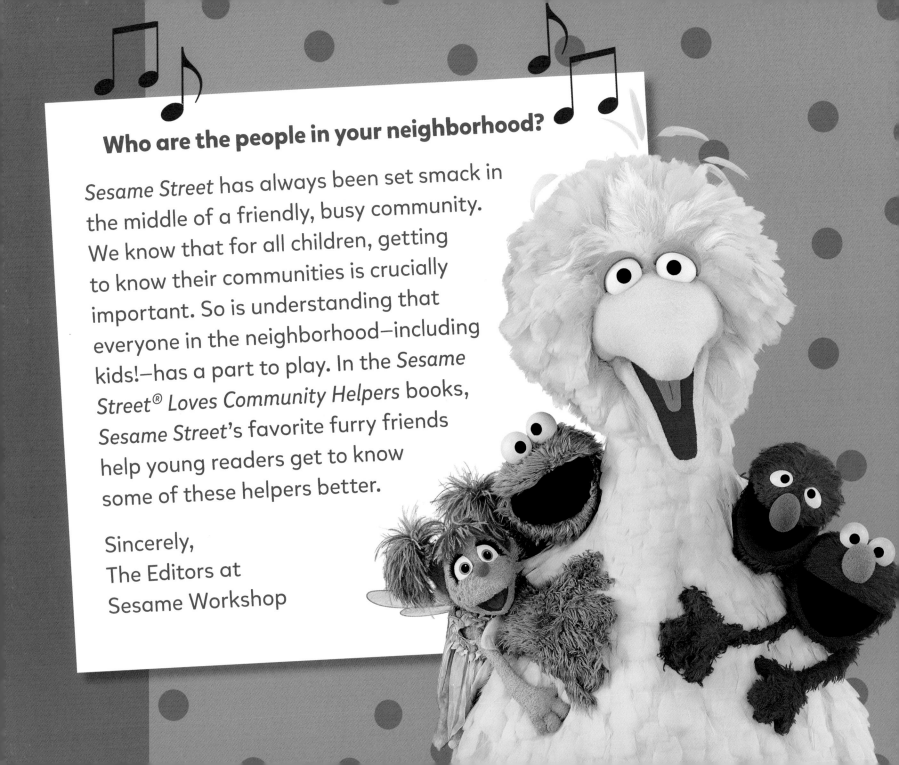

Who are the people in your neighborhood?

Sesame Street has always been set smack in the middle of a friendly, busy community. We know that for all children, getting to know their communities is crucially important. So is understanding that everyone in the neighborhood—including kids!—has a part to play. In the *Sesame Street® Loves Community Helpers* books, *Sesame Street*'s favorite furry friends help young readers get to know some of these helpers better.

Sincerely,
The Editors at
Sesame Workshop

Table of Contents

Big Jobs

Police officer jobs very important. They keep people safe.

On the Job

Police officers are community helpers. They work hard to help people follow laws.

Police officers help keep our neighborhood safe.

Police officers work
at police stations.

They also work in the community.

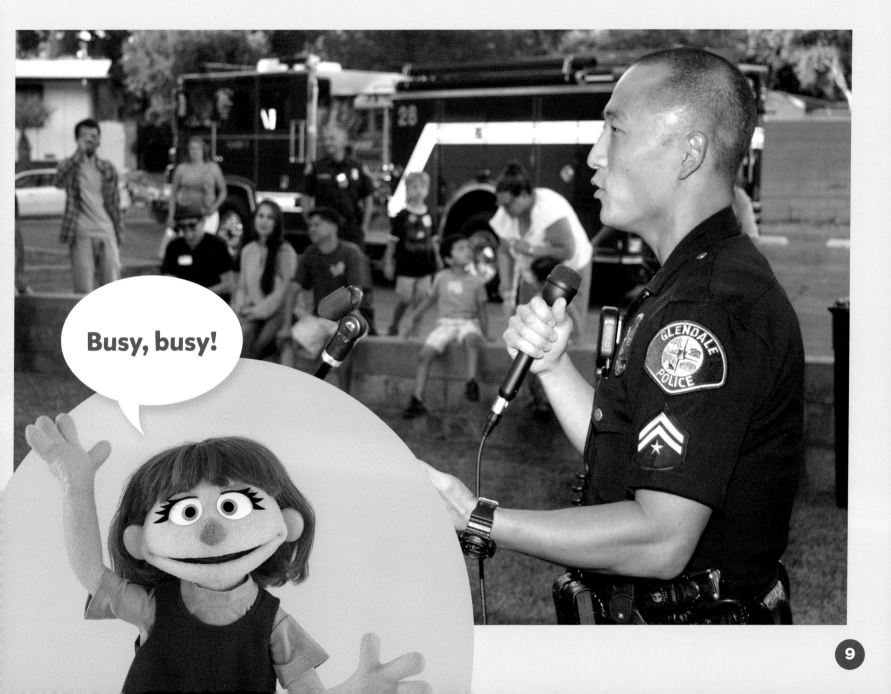

Busy, busy!

Some police officers walk or ride bikes. Others ride horses.

Let police animals do their work. Ask first if you want to pet them.

Many officers drive police cars.

A police car has flashing lights and makes loud sounds.

Some lights blue like me.

Or red like Elmo!

This helps officers get to places quickly when there's an emergency.

Police officers wear special uniforms.

Police officers work together.

Police officers are a team!

16

They work with the community too.

Police officers help people follow the laws.

They make sure people don't drive too fast.

Police officers try to keep people safe.

Officers help people who are hurt.

They can help if you get lost too.

Can you tell me how to get to Sesame Street?

Police dogs can smell very well. They sniff for people who are lost.

Police dogs are hard workers.

Officers help during emergencies. They tell people what to do and where to go.

Police officers are brave.

Police officers work hard every day!

Their job is to keep us all safe.

Thank You, Police Officers!

Now it your turn! Write thank-you note to police officers.

Dear Police Officers,

Thank you for keeping our community safe. Me like when you walk down street and say hello to everybody.

Your friend,

Cookie Monster

29

Picture Glossary

community: a place where people live and work

emergency: a time when people need help right away

laws: rules to follow in a community

stations: the buildings where police officers work

Read More

Bellisario, Gina. *Police Officers in My Community.* Minneapolis: Lerner Publications, 2019.

Gaertner, Meg. *Police Officers.* Minneapolis: Pop! 2019.

Leaf, Christina. *Police Officers.* Minneapolis: Bellwether Media, 2018.

Index

Photo Acknowledgments

Additional image credits: Simone Hogan/Shutterstock.com, p. 5; kali9/Getty Images, pp. 6, 12, 14, 16; Andersen Ross Photography Inc/Getty Images, pp. 7, 30; Darrin Klimek/Getty Images, pp. 8, 30; DnHolm/Getty Images, p. 9; Roberto Galan/Getty Images, p. 10; Bastiaan Slabbers/Getty Images, p. 11; Christian Mueller/Shutterstock.com, pp. 13, 30; aijohn784/Getty Images, pp. 15, 29; UpperCut Images/Getty Images, p. 17; Imagesbybarbara/Getty Images, pp. 18, 30; SDI Productions/Getty Images, pp. 19, 25; KatarzynaBialasiewicz/Getty Images, p. 20; RyanJLane/Getty Images, p. 21; jtyler/Getty Images, p. 22; X2Photo/Getty Images, p. 23; kaarsten/Getty Images, p. 24; Hill Street Studios/Getty Images, p. 26; Ronnie Kaufman/Getty Images, p. 27.

Cover: Hill Street Studios/Getty Images.

For the students at St. John Vianney School

Copyright © 2021 Sesame Workshop. ® Sesame Street.® and associated characters, trademarks and design elements are owned and licensed by Sesame Workshop. All rights reserved.

International copyright secured. No part of this book may be reproduced, stored in a retrieval system, or transmitted in any form or by any means—electronic, mechanical, photocopying, recording, or otherwise—without the prior written permission of Lerner Publishing Group, Inc., except for the inclusion of brief quotations in an acknowledged review.

Lerner Publications Company
An imprint of Lerner Publishing Group, Inc.
241 First Avenue North
Minneapolis, MN 55401 USA

For reading levels and more information, look up this title at www.lernerbooks.com.

Main body text set in Mikado Medium.
Typeface provided by HVD Fonts.

Editor: Allison Juda **Designer:** Emily Harris **Photo Editor:** Rebecca Higgins
Lerner team: Martha Kranes

Library of Congress Cataloging-in-Publication Data
Names: Schuh, Mari C., 1975- author.
Title: All about police officers / Mari Schuh.
Description: Minneapolis : Lerner Publications, [2021] | Series: Sesame street loves community helpers | Includes bibliographical references and index. | Audience: Ages 4–8 | Audience: Grades K–1 | Summary: "Sesame Street loves community helpers. And when it comes to keeping the community safe, police officers are the community helpers to call. Cookie Monster and his friends help young readers learn all about police officers."– Provided by publisher.
Identifiers: LCCN 2019041608 (print) | LCCN 2019041609 (ebook) | ISBN 9781541589988 (Library Binding) | ISBN 9781728400952 (eb pdf)
Subjects: LCSH: Police—Juvenile literature.
Classification: LCC HV7903 .S38 2021 (print) | LCC HV7903 (ebook) | DDC 363.2–dc23

LC record available at https://lccn.loc.gov/2019041608
LC ebook record available at https://lccn.loc.gov/2019041609

Manufactured in the United States of America
1-47508-48052-12/2/2019